Copyright MorningStar Publishers

All rights reserved. No part of this book may be reproduced without written permission of the copyright owner, except for the use of limited quotations for the purpose of book reviews.

The Wheel of The Year

celebrating

Forward

This pamphlet will provide a good understanding of Mabon, the seventh of the eight Festivals of the Wheel of the Year and the way it is celebrated. Each of the eight festival have been extracted from the guide book, 'The Wheel of the Year. A beginners guide to celebrating the traditional pagan festivals of the year.' New suggestions on your celebrations available only in these pamphlets have been added. If you are new to the Craft this selection of pamphlets will give you a solid base from where you can increase your understanding of the Craft and its many branches. For the more knowledgeable they will provide tried and tested ways to celebrate each of the eight Sabbats of the Wheel in a meaningful and fulfilling way other than in a formal Circle.

Included in each pamphlet are lists of correspondences, guided meditation, spells and seasonal activities linked to the festival. They have been crafted to resonate with the influences of the season and are the result of many years of personal celebration of The Wheel. Although I have worked within a group, my true path lies as a Solitary. I have accordingly aimed this book primarily at the Solitary Practitioner.

These Festivals are ancient, there is no doubt about that, but today, out of necessity, we often find we need to bring them in line with the parameters of modern life. Some of the practices and activities which would otherwise be impractical I have made more accessible by suggesting alternatives to traditional methods. Many of us no longer have access to open hearths and giant bonfires for example, so I have offered the alternatives I have found equally effective.

Life could be perilous for our ancestors and each festival marked a stepping stone from one seasonal change to the next.

Most of us no longer depend on the observance of the seasons to survive but the Wheel continues to turn and in doing so it demonstrate the astounding power of nature and its relentless progress. It reveals to us a power beyond our control yet one we can tap into. A power which is in the hands of the Divine. It instils in us a sense of awe and gratitude. For most, this gratitude expresses itself in the desire both to show appreciation and use that cosmic power to enrich not only our own lives but the world around us.

My hope is that these pamphlets will put your feet on the path of self-empowerment and instil a deeper appreciation of the staggering power of nature and the latent yet accessible power both within and around you. The Craft is not a 'dot to dot, follow my lead and do as I say' doctrine. It is a map. When you know the map and where to find what it is you need you can follow your chosen paths to it. Don't be told 'this way or no way'. Accept guidance, learn the routes then find your own way by your own self-empowerment.

Blessed Be

Introduction

For the purposes of this pamphlet we will be celebrating the Goddess as the Triple Goddess - Maiden, Mother and Crone, as worshipped since the 7th millennium BC. And her Consort, the Lord of the Greenwood, in two of his guises, the Oak King and the Holly King. He is a God of fertility, growth, death and rebirth.

I have suggested spells and activities at the times of the year when the seasonal influences are particularly sympathetic to that particular intent. I have also suggested that some activities be performed during your ritual. They do not have to be performed within a Sabbat Ritual; indeed there are those who believe the Sabbat Ritual is solely to celebrate the Sabbat not for personal spells and undertakings. If you choose to keep the Sabbat ritual exclusively for the Sabbat then the spells and activities can be performed separately or within an Esbat (Full Moon) Ritual but preferably while the Elemental Tides, the influences of the Sabbat, are still active. They are at their height from midday the day before until midday the day after the Sabbat. Before and after that time they slowly diminish until the adjoining Sabbat influences begin to take effect. I have provided lists of correspondences for this festival.

Correspondences are the colours, gems, herbs, incense, etcetera that are in tune with the season, your spell or your ritual's intent. For ease of use, and to allow you to select an alternative if you do not have the suggested item, I have included correspondence tables. With this you can link colour, gem stone, incense etcetera to the season or your spell. These are not meant to be exhaustive lists. There are many other choices available and no doubt you will add your own as you go.

Try not to get caught up on having just the right items, place, time, colour or any other of the endless conditions you think you need before you cast your spell or perform your ritual. Much of the power of your workings comes from your intent. Remember the old adage that *'if it be not found within then it be not found without'*. The power starts with you, the rest are aids, enhancements and focus items. See what works for you. Make notes then adapt and make more notes. Record which activities you chose to perform, the results of these activities and your thoughts, or suggestions, on how you can improve on it next time. There are workbooks available here which are specifically designed to work with 'The Wheel of the Year. *A beginners guide to celebrating the traditional pagan festivals of the year'.* They are perfect for creating your own Book of Shadows. The term 'Book of Shadows' simply refers to a record of things past; a shadow of all the activities you have performed and their results. It is particularly useful in allowing your power to grow and develop from your past experiences. It gives you your own personal guidelines as to what works for you. We are all unique.

When practising the Craft there is one major rule you should observe. It is known as the Witches Rede, sometimes known as the Wiccan Rede ('Wicca' believed to be derived from the ancient word for 'witch');

'If it harm none, do as you will.'

In the most basic of terms it seems to be saying you are free to do whatever you like. Sounds great! But it is not a licence to do as you want; it is a warning. It is reminding you that you must harm no-one and nothing. And not just in the practising of the Craft. It is a pointer to a way of life. A moment's thought will show you that it can be far more difficult to follow the Witches Rede than at first glance; everything you do affects something or someone somewhere. You will do well to observe the guidance of the Rede however if for no other reason than whatever you send out will come back to you sooner or later. In the Wheel of the Year what goes around, comes around.

The Wheel of the Year
A short history

Most of the Festivals, or Sabbats, date back to pre-Christian times and all are linked to the changing of the seasons. The festivals marked a time to pause and reflect on what had gone before and a time to prepare for what was to come. The ability to understand and prepare for the relentless changing of the weather and cycles of crops and animals was essential. With the festivals our ancestors celebrated endings and new beginnings; the end of the earth's dormant period and the return of fertility culminating in successful harvests; followed once more by the end of summer and the return of shorter days, cold weather and the conserving and gathering of strength for the winter.

Although the festivals are ancient and mark important events in the cycle of the year the first known introduction of the year as a wheel was given to us by Ross Nicholls in the 1950s. The Wheel of the Year demonstrates the cycle of birth, death and rebirth in its never-ending journey. As the Wheel turns the Circle of Life is represented by the eight Festivals. They are divided into four Greater and four Lesser Sabbats, alternating about six weeks apart. The four Greater Sabbats, also called the Cross-Quarters, are based on pre-Christian festivals and are known as Fire Festivals. They are held on fixed days of the year. The four Lesser Sabbats, also called the Quarters, are celebrated on the two Equinoxes and two Solstices and so are based on the position of the sun.

Within the four Lesser Sabbats the two Equinoxes are Ostara (also known as the Spring Equinox) and Mabon (the Winter Equinox). 'Equi' translated from Latin is 'equal'. While 'nox' is 'night' so 'equal night' referring to the equal number of hours of daylight and darkness. The Equinoxes are by default opposite each other on the Wheel of the Year.

The two Solstices are Litha and Yule. The word Solstice translates to 'sun standing'. It refers to the sun's position in the sky at its northernmost or southernmost extreme due to the tilt of the Earth's axis being most inclined toward or away from the sun. So it is a time when the apparent movement of the sun comes to a stop before reversing direction. So at Litha we have the longest day and at Yule we have the shortest day. Again the two Solstices are opposite each other on the Wheel.

These four Festivals divide the Wheel into Quarters.

The four Cross Quarters or Fire Festivals are the Greater Sabbats. They are pre-Christian and are based on cycles of life:-

Samhain; represents endings and beginnings.
Imbolc; a quickening.
Beltain; fertility.
Lammas, also known as Lughnasadh; harvest.

Each of these four Greater Sabbats is located midway between two Lesser Sabbats and at the turning points of the seasons. They cut across each quarter dividing the Wheel into eight parts. In this position these Sabbats look back to what was and look forward to what is to come.

It should be remembered that the eight festivals are attuned with the changing seasons of the year and so must change with where you are; the northern hemisphere being a direct opposite of the southern hemisphere. So though, for example, Beltain is celebrated on 1 May in the northern hemisphere, it is celebrated on 31 October in the southern hemisphere. I have given dates for both the northern and southern hemispheres. The southern hemisphere dates are in (brackets).

Festivals begin at sunset and last until the sunset of the next day.

Samhain - Greater Sabbat 31 October (1 May) - Root Harvest. Death and Rebirth. Communing with Ancestors. Cross Quarter. Fire Festival. Day of Power

Yule - Lesser Sabbat 20-21 December (21 June) - Winter Solstice. Return of the Oak King. Quarter. Longest night.

Imbolc - Greater Sabbat 1-2 February (2 August) - Purification. Quickening. Cross Quarter. Fire Festival. Day of Power.

Ostara - Lesser Sabbat 20-21 March (21 September) - Spring

Equinox. Spring Goddess. Quarter. Equal day and night.

Beltain - Greater Sabbat 1 May (31 October) - Fertility. Cross Quarter. Fire Festival. Day of Power.

Litha - Lesser Sabbat 20-21 June (21 December) - Summer Solstice. Return of the Holly King. Mid-summers Eve - offerings to the Fae. Quarter. Longest day.

Lammas - Greater Sabbat 1-2 August (2 February) - Bread Harvest. Cross Quarter. Fire festival. Day of Power.

Mabon - Lesser Sabbat 20-21 September (21 March) - Autumn Equinox, Vine Harvest. Quarter. Equal day and night.

Mabon
20-21 September (21 March)

Mabon is one of the Lesser Sabbats. It is a Quarter day midway between Lammas and Samhain. It is the Autumn Equinox which means that light and dark are once more equal, just as they were in Oestara which lies directly opposite on the Wheel of the Year. So Mabon is symbolic of equality and balance. Now however, it is the long nights and short days of winter which are approaching.

In the legend of Demeter and Persephone, Demeter has returned her daughter, Persephone, to the underworld to continue her teachings from Hades. Bereft at her loss Demeter halts the new growth and remains in mourning, awaiting the time her daughter will be returned to her at Oestara.

Mabon is a time to look back on the year that has been and to reflect on the changes taking place as darkness increases and temperatures fall. Farmers of the past and of the present prepare the earth and plant the winter wheat. It needs to be well established to survive the rigours of winter so timing is vital.

Though Mabon was not celebrated by the ancient Celts, the Anglo-Saxons referred to this month as Holy Month. The reasons for this and their practices are all mostly lost in time. Just like its partner, Oestara (the Summer Equinox), Mabon was only recently given its name. Previously it was simply known as the Autumn Equinox. The name Mabon was borrowed from the Welsh God, Mabon, the Son of Modred. Mabon means 'Great Son'. It is difficult to link the Autumn Equinox to the Welsh God unless you consider Mabon's life. He was kidnapped at the age of three to be rescued much later by King Arthur. So his life has come to represent the strength of survival and wisdom of age. The Autumn Equinox is a time when the earth had been reborn from the previous year, grown, flourished and then aged. It has experienced much and could be considered to have gained wisdom. It is now in its final phase before a new year begins at Samhain.

Mabon is the second harvest. The Christian churches are full with the offerings of the harvest festival. It is a time for reflection and giving thanks to the sun that poured its life into the crops being gathered and stored. We celebrate the Goddess as she passes from Mother to Crone and the Holly King, her Consort, who is gaining power and bringing rest and regeneration to the land.

The Mabon Altar

For a Mabon ritual dress your Altar in an autumnal coloured Altar cloth such as red, orange, maroon, gold, brown or russet. Decorate it with symbols of plenty and hidden life such as pinecones, grain, acorns, apples, pomegranates and seeds. Drape it with sprigs of hazel and vines of ivy. Add bunches of dried herbs, sunflowers or autumn leaves.

Suggested Activities for Mabon

Mabon can be recognised in other ways than in a formal ritual. Thank the land for its bounty by perhaps scattering offerings in a harvested field. Or honour the trees by making a symbolic offering such as placing a small fertiliser stick or a handful of plant food at its base. Prepare for the rebirth of the land by collecting seeds, gather and dry herbs or maybe try your hand at wine making with the harvested fruit and berries. If none of that appeals then a simple walk in the woods or park to breathe in the change of seasons as the land prepares for the coming darkness can help you find inner balance.

Mabon is the time for spell work concerning protection, self-confidence and prosperity. As light and dark are equal so spells for harmony and balance are particularly appropriate now.

Seasonal food
Celebrate the harvest with a feast that includes nuts, root vegetables, apples, pomegranates, nut and seed bread, grains and seeds such as sesame seeds, sunflower seeds and pumpkin seeds.

Mabon Correspondences

<u>Crystals and Gems</u>: Rich autumn colours like banded agate, carnelian, red jasper, onyx, amber, and tiger's-eye.
<u>Element</u>: Water
<u>Incense</u>: Myrrh, rose, honeysuckle.
<u>Flora</u>: Fern, honeysuckle, pine, and roses.
<u>Herbs</u>: Cinnamon, pine, sage, sweet-grass, ginger and all herbs. A good choice for a Mabon mix would be myrrh, sage, hibiscus and rose petals.
<u>Tree</u>: Apple.
<u>Colours</u>: Deep orange, burgundy, brown.
<u>Animals</u>: Salmon.
<u>Tarot Card</u> - Judgement: Representing the Harvest. Reaping rewards of labour. Rebirth. New awakenings.

Spells and Magical Workings for Mabon

The year has gained wisdom and is aging gracefully. It sits contentedly like a great Dragon amongst its bounteous wealth. It is benevolent and gracious. Spells for wisdom, courage, self-confidence and protection would be particularly powerful now. Or tap into the wealth all around you with a spell for prosperity. And as light and dark are equal it is a good time for spell work concerning harmony and balance.

A Spell to Boost Self-Confidence
This spell will give you a boost of courage if you have a difficult time coming up or if life seems to be closing doors in your face and you need that extra push to get things moving again. Though the tide of Mabon is particularly favourable for boosting self-confidence you could perform this spell at any time of the year. If you repeat it over several days it will greatly increase the affect. You could even make it a daily mantra with or without the red candle and herbs. The best time to perform this spell is at dawn preferably or at noon. If you want to burn herbs or essential oil then choose from fennel, yarrow or thyme. Add a pinch of dragon's blood to it if you can to enhance the power. Put a purple or red-toned coneflower (Echinacea) on your altar or desk. If you like you can wear it in your hair or pin it to your lapel. Coneflowers are easy to grow and are a delight in the garden. Make a note to yourself to buy some seed and prepare the ground for a big patch of beautiful coneflowers for next year.
For this spell you will need;
A mirror
A red candle
The herb of your choice if you intend to use one - fennel, yarrow or thyme or a mixture.

Light the candle and look at yourself in the mirror and say;

I am a Child of the strong Earth and of the Gods of old
I am a shining light and loved by the Devine

I am Worthy, I am Strong, I am Bold
The courage of the Dragon is mine.

Repeat this three times or three times three or as many times as you feel is right. Then snuff or blow out the candle and say;

I send light to make this right.

*****

<u>A Protection Pouch.</u>
There are times for whatever reason, we need to put ourselves into a situation where we know we will not feel completely at ease; coming home on a dark night, looking for a much loved lost pet, taking a trip that is unavoidable but daunting. Whatever it is this protection pouch can help. Although this is a good time for protection spells it would be little good if it were the only time of the year when you can create one. Like most spells it can be performed at any time of the year though this one would be best renewed or recharged every month at the new moon.
The best time to do this spell is at dawn.
You will need;
A spell candle in black, dark blue or white. A small pouch or circle of cloth in black or dark blue.
A ribbon or thread in black or dark blue to tie the cloth.
One stone from the following list; agate, amethyst, citrine, carnelian, clear quartz, or jade.
A pinch of rock-salt in a twist of greaseproof paper or tinfoil
A herb from the following list; angelica, basil, bay, fennel, rosemary or sage. Or you could use a small piece of dogwood.
Essential oil or incense-stick from the following list; bay, frankincense, honeysuckle, lotus, violet, rosemary or sandalwood.

If you are doing this spell for a loved one then have something of theirs with you while you work the spell. You need of course to enter their name in the place of 'me' in the spell. As the best time to do this spell is at dawn it is unlikely that it will be done in a full ritual. So collect the things you need the night before.
At dawn light the candle. Heat the essential or light the incense stick if you are using them. Find the still place inside of you. Know that you

are worthy. Know you have the power to ask and it will be given. Open your eyes and one by one put the items into the pouch or circle of material. As you do so repeat three times;

Amulet of power with stone and salt and flower
Guard me/... in times of need
Protect me/... from misdeed

Bunch the material into a bag and tie the top with the ribbon or thread. Finish it with three knots. As you tie the knots say;

I call upon the ancient power
On this day and in this hour
To charge this spell and guide it well.

Keep the pouch with you in your pocket or bag or briefcase or give it to your loved one to carry with them.

*****

At Mabon the harvests are in and the bounty of the land safely stored. Tap into the tide of plenty with this fast cash spell for times of immediate and urgent need.

Spell for Cash Fast
This is a simple spell and is designed to bring small amounts of cash to you in a rush when the need is urgent.
You will need;
A pre-practiced sigil outlining your need. Something like; 'fast cash' or 'money fast'. There are instruction on how to make a sigil and a sigil wheel for creating one in part three of this book. To make life a bit easier for you I have put a downloadable full sized sigil wheel on my blog at; http://maureen-murrish.blogspot.co.uk/
A green candle
Some basil essential oil
A few drops of almond or olive oil
Boline, orange-stick or burnt match, to inscribe the candle.
Incense is not essential to the spell but if you would like to burn some chose from cedar-wood, myrtle or orange.

Put a drop of basil essential oil into the almond or olive oil and mix with the Boline, orange-stick or match. As you do so visualise the cash being put into your hand.

Now take the stick or Boline and at the top of the candle where it will burn first, inscribe your sigil. As you do so repeat;

Herb of Basil hear my call
Bring fast cash from high and low
Bring joy and health but first of all
Bring me wealth to make it so

Now while still chanting dip you finger into the basil anointing-oil and coat the candle then put it into the holder. Light the candle and continue your chant until the candle has burned down and the sigil melted. You can see it is important for this spell to use a slender spell candle. If you only have a chunky candle you could stop chanting after five or ten minutes and allow the candle to burn down somewhere safe to melt the sigil. Make sure you put the sigil at the top of the candle where it will burn soonest. Perhaps you could meditate while it burns and visualise the money coming to you. Remember to visualise the desired results not the need!

This spell is best repeated over several days. You can re-use the chunky candle and the oil. Save the oil in a glass vial or something similar, preferably with a plastic or cork stopper as metal reacts to essential oil. And if there is still some candle left then you can save it to use in the future but only use it for this same spell if the need arises again.

Mabon Meditation

This meditation is to help balance the seven main Chakras. There is a brief chapter on Chakras and a suggested reading list for more information at the back of this book.

Prepare to meditate in the usual way. Breathe deeply, hold then exhale. Each time you exhale feel yourself getting more and more relaxed. Release the knots from you muscles. Allow your mind to become calm and still. Remind intrusive thoughts and worries that they haven't been forgotten but this is your time and they will be tended to very soon.

When you are ready visualise your forest around you. What kind of day is it? Or is it evening? The sounds of the forest comfort you and with a deepening sense of relaxation you follow a path you have never seen before. It leads you to a great tumble of stones and soil. Trees have taken root amongst the boulders and low plants form great cushions of green amongst them. You begin to wonder how you are to get past it when you see an opening to a cave. Step inside and look around. There is another opening at the other end of the cave and though it you can see a beach and hear the waves rolling softly onto the sand. The sound echoes around the cave and soothes you and you close your eyes to enjoy it. When you open them again you notice the walls of the cave are studded with different coloured gem-stones that are glowing with an inner light. There is a boulder in the middle of the cave, sit on it and listen to the ocean and feel the breeze as it passes through the cave. The walls and the boulder you are sitting on hold the heat of the day and you are warm and comfortable. As you look at the gem-studded walls the red stones begin to shine more brightly than the others until the whole cave is filled with a red light. Your Base Chakra the one at the base of your spine opens like a rosebud coming into full bloom. It is bright red like the light around you. Allow it to absorb as much of the light as it needs. After a short while the light in the cave changes from red to orange. Now you Base Chakra, which is linked to Earth Energies, closes and the Chakra located at the lower part of your abdomen opens. Like the light around you it is deep, joyful orange. The Abdomen Chakra is linked to spiritual strength and fortitude and it absorbs the orange light until it has its fill. When the light from the crystals change again, this time to yellow, the Abdominal Chakra closes and the Solar Plexus Chakra opens to receive the golden yellow light. Again allow it to absorb as much as it needs before the yellow rose closes until it is once more a bud. Now the light changes to a swirl of pink and green. Feel the rosebud of your Heart Chakra open and absorb the light until it can absorb no more. As it closes the light changes to a beautiful azure blue. Your Throat Chakra opens absorbing the colour and revitalising the Chakra that give clarity of communication. Again as the Throat Chakra absorbs its fill and closes the light changes this time to a deep rich purple. The rosebud Chakra at the centre of your forehead opens to admit it. This is the Third Eye Chakra and it is linked to psychic awareness and insight. Allow the purple light to enter the Chakra until it can absorb no more and then feel it close.

For the last time the light begins to change. All the crystals shine piercingly bright at once. The light around you becomes brilliant white. Your Crown Chakra at the top of your head and which resembles an unfolding lotus flower, opens and absorbs the pure white light. Feel it enter your Chakra and flood your body, bringing balance and harmony to all the other colours. This Crown Chakra is linked to Spiritual Union. When your Crown Chakra can absorb no more the light surrounding you fades and your Crown Chakra closes. Sit for a while and enjoy the feeling of balance and harmony. As you rise to leave the crystals embedded in the walls of the cave flash and sparkle as if biding you farewell. Walk back into the forest. Know you can return anytime to the cave whenever you need to bring balance and harmony into your life.

When you are ready, prepare to return to the room you are sitting in. Give yourself plenty of time to recover from this meditation. Notice how you feel. You ought to feel like this more often. And you can now you know how. Ground yourself with a drink and a bite to eat and write up your journal.

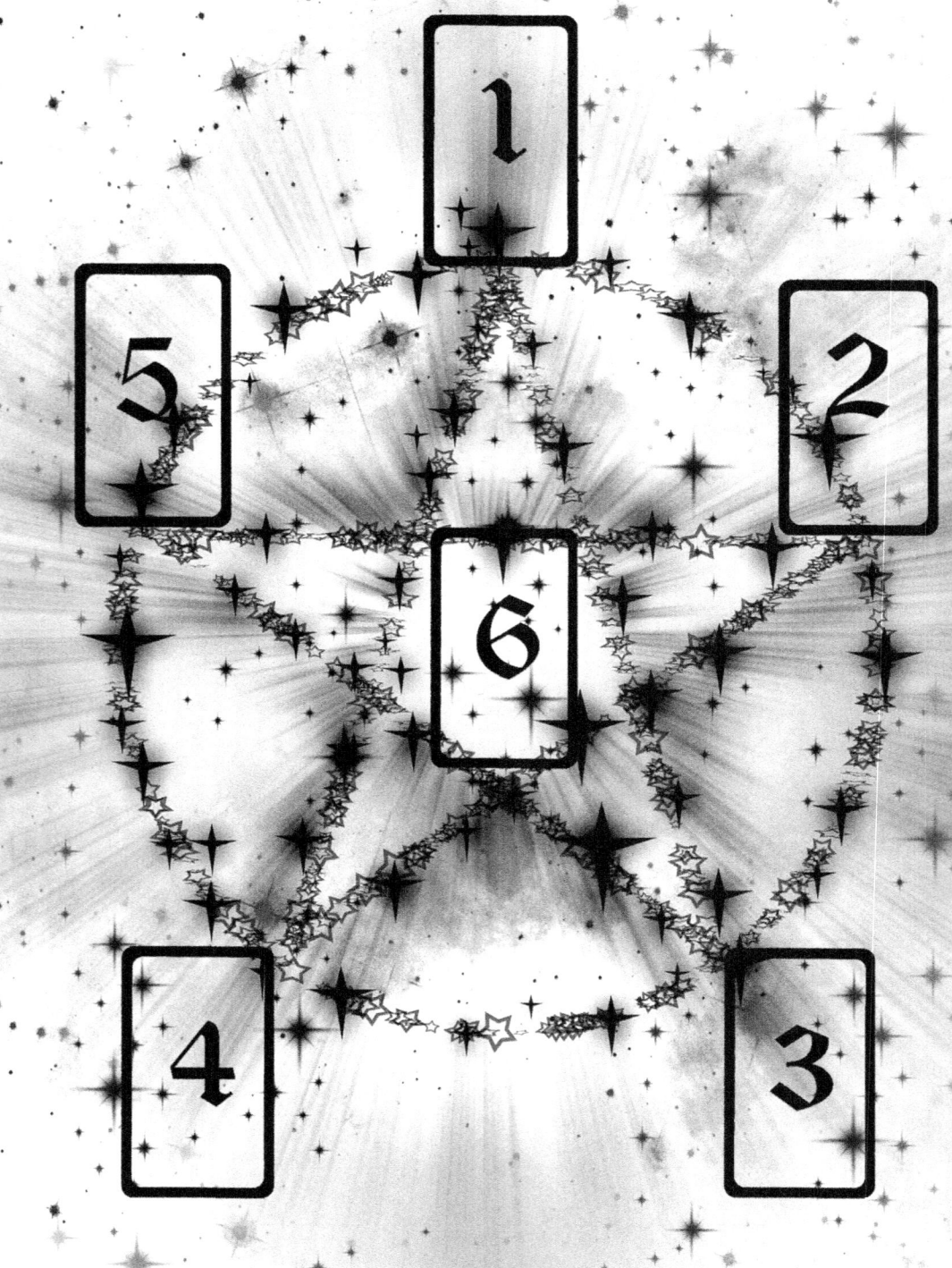

Mabon

Tarot Spread

1. What is out of balance in my family life?

2. How can I address that?

3. What is it that needs balancing in my work life?

4. What is the best way to bring the prosperity I seek?

5. What can I expect in my life between Lammas and Samhain?

6. What wisdom does the bountiful, Earth Dragon, have to share with me?

Honey Wheat Bread

Ingredients

2 cups warm water
1 Tbsp active dry yeast
1/3 cup of honey
3 cups whole wheat flour
1 tsp salt
¼ cup vegetable oil
2 tbsp butter
4 cups all -purpose flour

Makes 2 loaves

Method

Dissolve the yeast in the warm water. Add honey and mix well.
Stir in the whole wheat flour, salt, vegetable oil, and butter and mix until a stiff dough has formed. Gradually work the all-purpose flour into the mix, one cup at a time.
Turn the dough onto a lightly floured counter-top, and knead for about fifteen minutes. When it reaches the point where it's sort of elastic, shape it into a ball and place it into an oiled bowl. Cover with a warm, damp cloth, and allow to sit and rise until it's doubled in size -- usually about 45 minutes.

Punch the dough down and cut in half, so you can make two loaves of bread. Place each half in a greased loaf pan, and allow to rise. Once the dough has risen an inch or two above the top of the loaf pan, pop them in the oven. Bake at 375 for half an hour, or until golden brown at the top.
When you remove the loaves from the oven, allow to cool for about fifteen minutes before removing from the pan. If you like, brush some melted butter over the top of the hot loaves, to add a pretty golden glaze to them.

Recipe by Linda Rupp

Essential oil blend

Balancing body and mind

Some times you can just feel out of sorts – off balance and unsure. This blend of essential oils is designed to help balance both body and mind. Mabon, with its perfectly balanced light and dark is a perfect time to prepare it. Put a few drops on water in your oil burner as you meditate. Or drop some into your bathwater and lay back and breath in the healing steam. You can also put it in a base oil such as almond oil to use as perfume. As with any of these mixtures less is more so wear it sparingly.

Balance

2 drops of Lavender
2 drops of Cinnamon
2 drops of Sandalwood

Other books by M Murrish:-

Work books:

The Wheel of the Year: *A beginners guide to celebrating the traditional pagan festivals of the seasons.*

The Wheel of the Year: *A 1yr 3yr or 5 year work book and Journal for the pagan festivals.* (Companion workbook to: *A beginners guide to celebrating the traditional pagan festivals of the seasons.*)

Three Card Spread Tarot Journal: *Ideas for three card spreads including prompts with room for your detailed interpretation and outcome.*

I AM .... *A prompted motivational affirmation journal to increase self-esteem and self empowerment*

Family Tree Research Journal: *Family history fill-in charts and research forms in a handy and logically ordered workbook*

Weaving Project Planner and Journal: *Designed for the beginner or experienced weaver working on a rigid heddle, 4 or 8 sha   loom.*

Gardening Journal Monthly Planner: *Organise your garden week by week with detailed record sheets and a diary based log book.*

Novels:

The Bonding Crystal: *book one of the Dragon World Series. A fantasy adventure with dragons, sorcery, elves and goblins.*

The Missing Link: *book two of the Dragon World Series.* **The Forth Gate:** *book three of the Dragon World Series.* **The Lost Sorcerer:** *A novella*

Thank you for choosing this Journal. If you find it as useful and inspiring as we do please consider leaving a positive review on Amazon as it will help others to find it too.

Scan the QR code below to check out our other books, notebooks, journals and reference books.

https://maureenmurrish.com/

Printed in Great Britain
by Amazon